This book is a gift to all doctors in the world and Italy.
I hope that our beloved world will not infect any harm
or other pandemic. Mercy for all who died.
May God protect our world, all of our countries
, and all the thanks to the doctors who work
day and night for our lives

O

GUCCI
VERSACE
PRADA
MILANO
RALPH LAUREN
william shakespeare
THE TRAGEDY OF ROMEO AND JULIET
WILLIAM SHAKESPEARE

Italy

. if someone asked you about beauty ,
tell him about Italy
. if you love history ,you have to study
roman civilization
. in literature tell him about , romeo and juliet
and the legend william shakespeare
.Number one in super car
like lamborghini and ferrari
The land of love and beauty
(Verona , Venice , Rome)
the art here is reflected on our imagination
when we talk about leonardo da vinci
and michelangelo

1

The dark side
&
The bright side

The dark side

Apandemic

disease

economy

wars

Throughout history, mankind has known many black moments due to diseasesand epidemics that have killed
an enormous number of people. In addition to the black plague, which caused the demise of about a quarter
of the population of the Middle Ages and the London plague, which led to the death of more than 75 thousand in 1665
and the plague of Marseille, which finished over 100,000 people in 1720, Italy passed in the year 1629 a wave of plague
that emptied many cities from its inhabitants and caused
In the collapse of the greatness of some of them

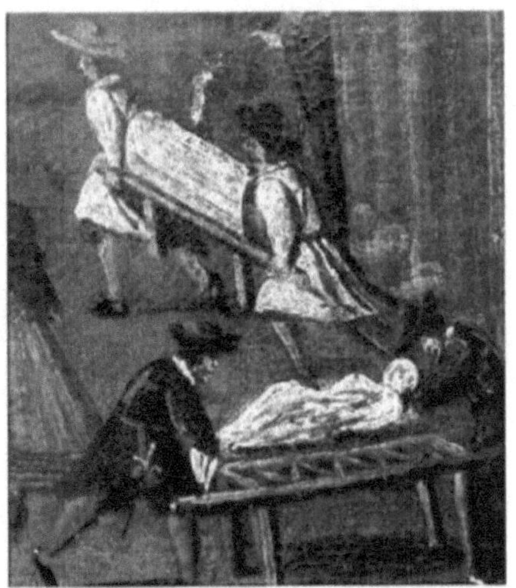

a side of one of the paintings that embodied the transport
of dead bodies from the streets during the plague that
rocked Italy

4

In the midst of the Thirty Years' War, which lasted between
1618 and 1648,German and French forces moved through
northern Italy, taking with them the bubonic plague epidemic
the Italian states.
According to many historians, the disease was recorded in 1629
in the city of Mantua, Lombardy. With their withdrawal
from northern and central Italy, soldiers of the Republic of Venice
contributed to spreading bubonic plague the rest of the cities

First plague wave

In addition, by October 1629 the city of Milan, Italy,
which had taken weeks of health measures to prevent
the spread of the disease, had reached the epidemic.
It deliberately isolated all suspicious cases,
created special places for patients,
restricted the movement of trade in its markets, and prevented
a significant percentage of German soldiers from entering it.

Meanwhile, these measures were not enough.
 By March 1630, Milan was shaken by the outbreak of
the first plague, which spread due to
 the events of the carnival of the city. During the
spring and summer of 1631, Milan witnessed a
second wave of plague, which left a huge ruin in it.

According to many sources, the bubonic plague
epidemic between 1629 and 1631 resulted in the
deaths of about 60,000 Milan residents, who
were then estimated at 130,000, equivalent to
46 percent of the city's population before the disaster began.

Disastrous results

And with Venice, the epidemic caused
catastrophic consequences, weakened
the city, exhausted its economy and lost
it as part of its global luster, causing the
death of 46,000 people, which is then
estimated to one third of the
population.

6

As for Verona, its losses were greater compared to the rest
of the Italian cities,where 33 thousand of its people died
due to illness,a number equivalent to 60 percent
of its population before the start of the plague.

Also, the epidemic reached a number of other
prominent Italian cities. In Florence, the
number of plague victims reached 9 thousand, and in
Bologna,the number of dead people
exceeded 15 thousand, which is equivalent to a quarter
of its population.

In their writings, a number of those who witnessed
the epidemic spoke about the spread of
dead bodies in the streets and the resort of some cities,
such as Venice and Milan, to isolate
patients and burn their clothes and property to prevent
the spread of the epidemic. The
Venetian authorities later moved to adopt other procedures,
as they collected significant
numbers of patients and exiled them outside the city
by isolating them in one of the nearby islands.

In addition, the bubonic plague epidemic that struck Italy
between 1629 and 1631 resulted in the deaths
of at least 230,000 of its residents, with negative
impacts on many of its states, which had an important
role in the regionover the past centuries.

A fictional drawing of
plague doctor over the past centuries

8

The first influenza pandemic in 1580

Although the first cases of influenza may have occurred among Greek soldiers who fought the Peloponnese in 430 BC, the first real flu pandemic appeared in the summer of 1580 in Asia, and the epidemic quickly spread through trade routes to Europe and North America. Although the death toll is unknown, at least 8,000 deaths have been reported in Rome alone.

This period witnessed the emergence of quarantine procedures and border checkpoints in Europe, and the first reference to influenza in scientific literature dates back to 1650, and is derived from the Italian word for "effect".

9

COVID_19 (CORONA VIRUS)

The virus officially began to circulate on February 20/2020
when a 38 years man underwent a medical examination at
hospital in Cudono in the northern Italian region of
Lombardy ,

Paglia is likely that virus patients have been
 treated as a seasonal flu,
and may have health facilities that hostthese patients
have become the transfusion sites,
 which helpedspread virus.
 The Italian northern regions such as Lombardy,
 Veneto, and Emilia-Romagna
, have been significantly affected by a large number
 of Korona's casualties throughout the country,
but are the world's largest
rate of 92 percent

10

WARS

wars that included independent Italy since 1861:

The Third Italian War of Independence (1866).

Rome annexation (September 20, 1870).

First Italian-Ethiopian War (1895--1896).

The Boxers Revolution (1899-1901).

The Ottoman Italian War (1911-1912).

World War I (1915-1918).

The Allies interfered in the Russian Civil War (1918-1920).

Occupation of Antalya (1918-1923).

The Corfu Crisis (1923).

The Second Italian-Ethiopian War (1935--1936).

The Italian invasion of Albania (1939).

World War II (1940-1945).

11

Economy of Italy

The economy of Italy is the 3rd-largest national
economy in theEuropean Union,
the 8th-largest by nominal GDP in the world, and the
12th-largest by GDP (PPP). Italy has a major advanced
 economy and [22] is a founding member of the European
Unionthe Eurozone, the OECD, the G7 and the G20. Italy is
 the eighth largest exporter in the world with $514 billion
exported in 2016. Its closest trade ties are with the other
countries of the European Union, with whom it conducts
 about 59% of its total trade.
The largest trading partners, in order of market share
 Despite these important achievements, the country's
economy today suffers from
structural and non-structural problems. Annual growth
rates have often been below the
EU average with Italy being hit particularly hard
by the late-2000s recession. Massive
government spending from the 1980s onwards
 has produced a severe rise in public debt.
In addition, Italian living standards have
 a considerable North–South divide: the average
GDP per capita in Northern and Central Italy
significantly exceeds the EU average, while
some regions and provinces in Southern Italy are
 dramatically below.[34] In recent years,
Italy's GDP per capita growth slowly caught-up with
the Eurozone average[35] while its
employment rate still lags behind; however, economists
 dispute the official figures because
of the large number of informal jobs (estimated between
10% and 20% of the labour force) that lift the inactivity

12

the bright side

Arts

Fashion

Brands

Civilization

Industry

13

Arts

One of the most famous countries in the world in art,
 paintings, international artists and museums,
and of course we know
 the artist Michelangelo, Titan and Leonardo Da Vinci
who left tothe world a great artistic legacy and
raised Italian art to a high level
 and in their footsteps many international and
contemporary artists followed.
 This was manifested in world famous paintings and
exquisite sculptures

Michelangelo Pistoletto began painting
 on mirrors in 1962, connecting painting
 with the constantly changing realities in
 which the work finds itself. In the later
 1960s he began bringing together rags
 with casts of omnipresent classica
l statuary of Italy to break down the
 hierarchies of "art" and common things.
 An art of impoverished materials I
s certainly one aspect of the definition
 of Arte Povera. In his 1967 Muretto di
straci (Rag Wall) Pistoletto makes an
 exotic and opulent tapestry wrapping
 common bricks in discarded scraps of
fabric.

14

Artists such as Jannis Kounellis and Mario Merz
attempted to make the experience of art more
immediately real while also more closely connecting
the individual to nature.

The leading sculptors from 1930-40 to
2000 included Marino Marini, Emilio
Greco, Pino Pascali, Mario Ceroli,
Giovanni e Arnaldo Pomodoro, Umberto Mastroianni,
Ettore Colla.

The leading painters from 1930-40 to
2000 included Alberto Savinio, Giorgio de Chirico,
Giorgio Morandi, Alberto Magnelli, Felice Casorati,
Roberto Melli, Corrado Cagli, Gianfilippo Usellini,
Pietro Annigoni, Renato Guttuso, Lucio Fontana,
Giovanni Capogrossi, Enrico Accatino, Antonio Donghi,
Oreste Carpi, Fausto Pirandello, Afro Basaldella, Alberto
Burri, Mimmo Rotella, Franco Nonnis, Domenico Gnoli,
Valerio Adami, Piero Manzoni, Emilio Tadini, Salvatore
Provino, Mino Argento.
A new breed of contemporary Italian
artist such as Gaspare Manos are
developing a more global language that
draws on a vast international personal
experience of life and culture stretching over several
continents and many
decades of travel. Such artist think locally and act globally,
like Rabarama who has been the first
Italian sculptor to collaborate with
the Cirque du Soleil. An equivalent in
Spain for example is the painter Miquel Barceló.

15

the most famous paintings and works
by Leonardo da vinci

16

by Leonardo da vinci

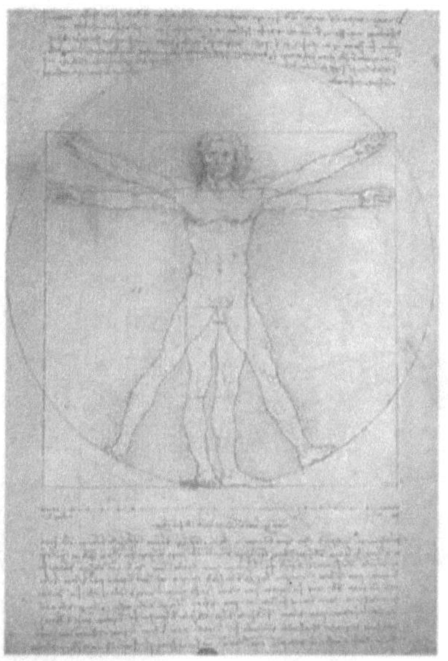

17

by michelangelo

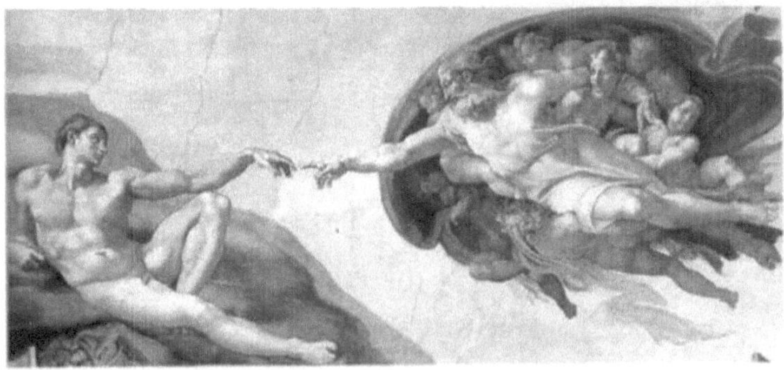

18

Super car

In 2014 Ferrari was rated the world's most powerful brand
 by Brand Finance.In June 2018, the 1964 250 GTO became
the most expensive car in history, setting an all-time record
 selling price of $70 million.
Fiat S.p.A. acquired 50% of Ferrari in1969 and expanded
its stake to 90% in 1988.In October 2014 Fiat Chrysler
Automobiles N.V. (FCA) announced its
intentions to separate Ferrari S.p.A. from
FCA; as of the announcement FCA owned 90% of Ferrari.
The separation began in October 2015 with a restructuring
that established Ferrari
N.V. (a company incorporated in the Netherlands) as
 the new holding company of the Ferrari group and the
subsequent sale by FCA of 10% of the
shares in an IPO and concurrent listing
of common shares on the New York Stock Exchange.
Through the remaining steps of the separation,
FCA's interest in Ferrari's business was distributed to
 shareholders of FCA,with 10% continuing to be owned by
 Piero Ferrari.The spin-off was completed on 3
 January 2016.   Throughout its history, the company has
been noted for its continued participation in racing,
 especially in Formula One, where it is the oldest
 and most successful racing team, holding
the most constructors championships
(16) and having produced the highest
number of drivers' championship wins
(15).Ferrari road cars are generally seen
 as a symbol of speed, luxury and wealth

19

lamborghini

Ferruccio Lamborghini, an
 Italian manufacturing magnate, founded
 Automobili Ferruccio Lamborghini S.p.A.
in 1963 to compete with established
 marques, including Ferrari. The
company was noted for using a rear mid-engine,
rear-wheel drive.
Lamborghini grew rapidly during its first decade, but
sales plunged in the wake of the 1973 worldwide financial
downturn and the oil crisis. The firm's ownershipchanged
 three times after 1973, including a bankruptcy in 1978.
 American Chrysler Corporation took control of Lamborghini
 in 1987 and sold it to Malaysian investment group Mycom
Setdco and Indonesian group V'Power
Corporation in 1994. In 1998, Mycom Setdco and V'Power
 soldLamborghini to the Volkswagen Group where it
 was placed under the control of the group's Audi division.
New products and model lines were
introduced to the brand's portfolio and
brought to the market and saw an
increased productivity for the brand. In
the late 2000s, during the worldwide financial crisis and
the subsequenteconomic crisis, Lamborghini's sales saw
a drop of nearly 50 percent.Lamborghini currently produces
the V12-powered Aventador and the V10-powered Huracán,
along withthe Urus SUV powered by a twin-turbo V8 engine
 In addition, the company produces V12 engines for offshore
powerboat racing. Lamborghini Trattori, founded in 1948 by
 Ferruccio Lamborghini, is headquartered in Pieve di Cento,
 Italy and continues to produce tractors.

20

Maserati

The company's headquarters are now in Modena, and its
 emblem is a trident.It has been owned by the Italian-
American car giant FIAT Chrysler Automobiles
(FCA) and FCA's Italian predecessor FIAT S.p.A. since 1993.
 Maserati was initially associated with Ferrari, which was
also owned by FCA until being spun off in 2015
, but more recently it has become part of the sports car group
 includingAlfa Romeo and Abarth. In May 2014,
 due to ambitious plans and product launches, Maserati
sold a record of over 3,000 cars in one month.This caused
them to increase production of the Quattroporte and
Ghibli models.In addition to the Ghibli and Quattroporte,
 Maserati offers the Maserati GranTurismo, the GranTurismo
 Convertible, the Maserati Levante
(the first ever Maserati SUV).Maserati has placed
 a production output cap at 75,000 vehicles globally

21

24

Tourism in Italy, which has one of the most beautiful cities
 in the world,
 which is visited by visitors from everywhere, such as Rome,
 famous for its
 history and its ancient and distinctive buildings,
 including the amphitheater,
 theaters, and antique museums.
Venice with lanes and entrances full of water and you can
 move around by boats
 calm waters that reflect the pictures of the magnificent
buildings on its side,

As for Romeo and Juliet Verona, the city of love and
 its beautiful buildings.
 which tourists come annually throughout the year
to enjoy its charming beauty.

22

Italy is one of the leading countries
in fashion design, alongside France,
the United States and the United Kingdom. Fashion has
 always been an important part of the country's cultural
 life and society, and Italians are wellknown for their
attention of dressing-upwell; "la bella figura", or good
impression, remains traditional.Italian fashion became
prominent duringthe 11th to 16th centuries, when artistic
development in Italy was at its peak. Cities such as Rome,
Palermo, Venice, Milan, Naples, Florence and Vicenza
started to produce luxury goods, hats, cosmetics, jewelry and
rich fabrics. From the 17th century to the early 20th, Italian
 fashion lost its importance and lustre and Europe's
main trendsetter became France, with the great popularity
of French fashion; this is due to the luxury dresses which
were designed for the courtiers of Louis XIV.However,
since the 1951–53 fashion soirées held by Giovanni Battista
 Giorgini in Florence, the "Italian school" started
to compete with the French haute couture, and labels such
as Ferragamo and Gucci began to contend with Chanel
and Dior. In 2009, according to the Global Language
Monitor, Milan, Italy's centre of design, was ranked the
 top fashion capital of the world, and Rome was ranked
fourth,and, although both cities fell in subsequent rankings
, in 2011, Florence entered as the 31st world fashion capital
. Milan is generally considered to be one of the "big four"
global fashion capitals, along with New York City, Paris,
 and London; occasionally, the "big five" also includes Rome.
Italian fashion is linked to the most generalized concept of "
Made in Italy"

23

, a merchandise brand expressing excellence of creativity and craftsmanship. Italian luxury goods are renowned for the quality of the textiles and the elegance and refinement of their construction. Many French, British and American high-top luxury brands (such as Chanel, Dior, Balmain and the main line of Ralph Lauren) also rely on Italian craft factories, located in highly specialized areas in the metropolitan area of Naples and in the centre-north of Italy (Tuscany, Marche, Veneto and Piedmont), to produce parts of their apparel and accessories.

The nonprofit association that co-ordinates and promotes the development of Italian fashion is the National Chamber of Italian Fashion (Camera Nazionale della Moda Italiana), now led by Carlo Capasa. It was set up in 1958 in Rome and now is settled in Milan and represents all the highest cultural values of Italian fashion. This association has pursued a policy of organisational support aimed at the knowledge, promotion and development of fashion through high-profile events in Italy and abroad.

24

Examples of major Italian fashion houses
focused on both menswear and womenswear, but also
 accessories, are: Giorgio Armani,Byblos (designed by
 Manuel Facchini), Bottega Veneta (designed by Daniel Lee),
Roberto Cavalli, Costume National, Brunello Cucinelli
 Diesel (created by Andreas Melbostad
as long as the Black Gold line is concerned),Dolce & Gabbana,
Etro, Fay (headed by Arthur Arbesser), Fendi
(previously directed by Karl Lagerfeld for women's clothes
and ready to wear and by Silvia Venturini
Fendi for accessories and men's lines), Salvatore Ferragamo
(designed by Paul Andrew for women's shoes and
apparel and Guillame Meilland for men's lines),
Fiorucci, Frankie Morello, Genny (designed by Sara
Cavazza Facchini), Gucci (directed by Alessandro Michele),
 Hogan, Iceberg (directed by James Long), Kiton, La Perla
(directed by Julia Haart), Loro Piana, Marni (founded by
ConsueloCastiglioni and now directed by Francesco Risso),
 Antonio Marras, Missoni, Moncler, Moschino (dir
ected by Jeremy Scott), MSGM
(directed by Massimo Giorgetti),
N°21 (created by Alessandro Dell'Acqua), Prada, Richmond,
Ermanno Scervino, Tod's (designed by
 Andrea Incontri regarding men's
lines), Trussardi, Valentino (directed by
Pier Paolo Piccioli) and Versace (directed
by Donatella Versace) to name the most significant.

25

Examples of major fashion brands which are specialized
mainly at womenswear (and also accessories for women)
are Agnona (designed by Simon Holloway), Luisa Beccaria,
Laura Biagiotti, Blumarine (created by Anna Molinari),
Chiara Boni la petit robe, Capucci (directed by Mario Dice),
Alberta Ferretti, Elisabetta
Franchi, Giamba (created by designer Giambattista Valli),

Krizia (founded by Mariuccia Mandelli and now art
directored by Zhu Chongyun), Max Mara
(created by Laura Lusuardi), Miu Miu
(founded and directed by Miuccia Prada), Philosophy
(directed by Lorenzo Serafini),
Emilio Pucci, Simonetta Ravizza,
Mila Schon and Twin-set Milano whilst the most important
luxury houses which focus only on menswear and
accessories for men are Brioni, Canali, Caruso, Corneliani,
Lardini, MP Massimo Piombo, Stefano Ricci, Ermenegildo
Zegna (directed by Alessandro Sartori) and Pal Zileri
(created by Rocco Iannone).

26

In the end, we should thank the famous Italian food that all the world knows, like the pizza that everyone loves, young and old, and delicious spaghetti. The Italian cuisine is varied, delicious and famous. It was and still is one of the best kitchens, adding taste and taste to all recipes in the world

27